Slomo's Secret Treasure

Book 2: A Blending Book by Jennifer Makwana

Collect all five books in the Alpha-Mania™ book series!

Based on the Alpha-Mania™
program created by Ruth Rumack
www.ruthrumack.com

How to Use This Book

Reading picture books to children provides them with many of the skills necessary for school readiness. Children learn even more when they are actively involved in the stories they read.[1] The Alpha-Mania™ books are designed to do just that.

There are four elements to each Alpha-Mania™ book:

The first element is the story itself, which follows the Alpha-Mania™ characters on an exciting adventure that both children and parents will enjoy.

The second element incorporates a different phonological awareness skill into the storyline of each book. Phonological awareness is the ability to recognize, reflect on, and eventually manipulate the sounds of spoken language.[2] This includes:

- Rhyming
- Blending (combining individual sounds to make words)
- Alliteration (repetition of the first sound in a group of words)
- Segmenting (separating words into individual sounds)
- Manipulating sounds within words

These skills are important predictors of reading success. Research on early reading strategies shows that phonological awareness is an important foundation in helping children learn to read.[3] Children who develop an understanding that words can be broken up into sounds tend to become better readers.[4] The Alpha-Mania™ books provide opportunities for your child to become actively engaged with both the individual stories and the specific phonological awareness skills practiced throughout the books.

The third element of the Alpha-Mania™ books focuses on sound-symbol correspondence. This element is embedded in the illustrations of the story. Sound-symbol correspondence, also known as *phonics*, is the ability to relate speech sounds to the letters or symbols that represent those sounds.[5] When you read the Alpha-Mania™ stories to your child, refer to the guide at the bottom of the page to hunt for objects or letters in the illustrations. For example, the guide may show a picture of an object and ask your child to hunt for the first letter of the object in the illustration. Additionally, the guide may ask your child to find an object that starts with the sound made by a particular letter. It is important to make the distinction between the name of the letter, the sound of the letter, and the symbol that represents the letter. As you complete this aspect of the book with your child, be sure to refer to both the *name* of the letter ("The name of this letter is M (/em/).") and the *sound* made by that letter ("It makes the sound /m/.").* For example, when you see the picture of the map, ask, "What *sound* does *map* begin with?" Then ask, "What *letter* makes that sound?"

You may choose to complete this part of the story as you read, but you may also decide to revisit it after the story is complete. The decision should be made based on your child's level of interest as well as his or her ability to focus on both aspects of the book.

The fourth element of the Alpha-Mania™ books includes additional activities for you and your child. These activities are meant to reinforce the particular phonological awareness skill of the book as well as practice other early literacy skills, such as letter formation and phonics. These activities can be played at any time, whether you are reading the story or not. They are simply a collection of fun and educational things to do when you have about fifteen minutes to spend with your child.

The phonological awareness focus of this book is blending. One of the most important precursors to reading is an understanding that words are made up of individual phonemes, or sounds.[6] When children blend, they must listen to a sequence of separately spoken phonemes, and then combine the phonemes to form a word.[7] This awareness allows children to see that letters of the alphabet correspond to the sounds in words.[8] Blending can be practiced in a progression of four stages:

1. Compound Words (say "jig…saw" and child blends words into "jigsaw")
2. Syllables (say "ba…na…na" and child blends syllables into "banana")
3. Onset and Rime (say "j…ump" and child blends parts into "jump")
4. Individual Phonemes (say "sssuuunnn" and child blends sounds into "sun")

A thorough understanding of blending sounds into words is critical for later, more difficult concepts such as segmenting sounds.[9]

In this book, the Alpha-Maniacs meet a slow-speaking sloth that often stretches the sounds in words. As you read, it is important to pronounce the sloth's speech correctly to allow your child a chance to blend the sounds and discover the word. The sounds that need to be held, or stretched, will be repeated in the spelling. For example, when the sloth says the word *map*, it will be written as *mmmaaap*. This indicates that you should stretch both the /m/ sound, and the /a/ sound, but not the /p/ sound. (Certain "quick" sounds should not be stretched - see Appendix A for a complete explanation of quick and stretchy sounds.) In addition, when you see an ellipsis (…), this indicates you should pause before continuing with the rest of the word. For example, when the sloth says the word *someone*, it will be written as *some…one*. This indicates that you should pause between the *some* and *one*. Sometimes the story will ask questions of your child, for example, *"Where do the Alpha-Maniacs need to go next?"* You may need to repeat some of the stretched words in the text so that your child has a chance to practice blending the words on his or her own. You may find it somewhat difficult to read initially, but stick with it. Your child will likely enjoy your slow-talking sloth voice, so take your time and have fun with it!

*Note: It is important to pronounce the sounds of each letter correctly.
See Appendix A for a guide to the correct pronunciation of letter sounds.

The Letter Lagoon is a magical place. It's a place where towering cliffs, mysteriously carved with letters, rise out of the crystal blue water. It's a place where adventure hides behind every twisted tree and rugged rock. It's a place where you never know what might happen next.

It's also the home of the Alpha-Maniacs.

Alex, Eddie, Izzy, Olly, and Umber call themselves the Alpha-Maniacs because they *love* letters! In fact, they love letters so much, even their shirts have letters on them.

Can you guess who is who?

Nearly a month had passed since the Alpha-Maniacs' first encounter with real pirates.

"Do you think Captain Ray and his crew will find the treasure on their map?" wondered Izzy as they strolled along the beach looking for seashells.

"Of course they'll find it," Eddie insisted. "We taught them everything we know."

"I wish we were the ones out searching for treasure," sighed Alex. "We could sure use a little adventure around here today."

Find the letters that these pictures begin with...

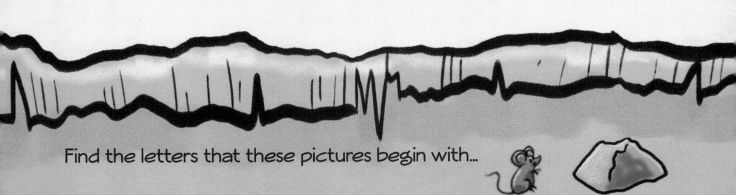

"You want adventure, Alex? I'll race you to that cave over there," Olly yelled. Alex dropped her shells and raced after him.

"Watch out for that log!" Umber called out just before Olly and Alex landed in a heap in the sand.

Find *objects* that start with the sounds...

B F

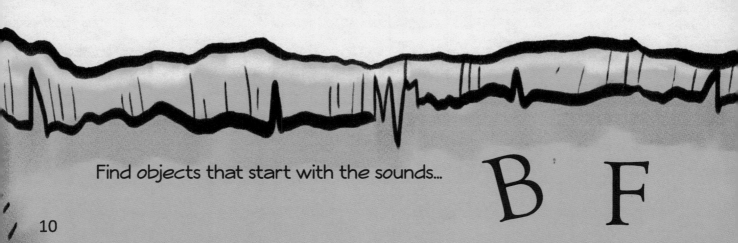

10

When the others caught up to them, Olly and Alex were staring in disbelief at the sand.

"What is it? Are you guys okay?" inquired Izzy.

Everyone leaned in to see a weathered old scroll poking out from under the driftwood.

Find the letters that these pictures begin with...

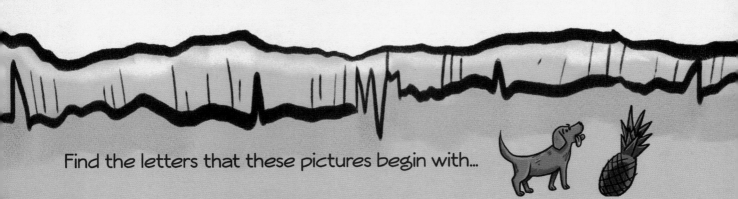

"Is that what I think it is?" Eddie stammered.

Umber unrolled the scroll. "Well, if you think it's a treasure map, upon my initial inspection, it does appear to have some of the elements that are typical to a map of..."

"Of course it's a treasure map, Umber!" Olly cut in.

"There's something very familiar about this map." Izzy noted.

"You're right, Izzy," Alex agreed. "I just don't know what it could be."

Suddenly, Eddie snatched up the map and held it out in front of him.

"I don't believe it! This is a map of Alpha-Mania Island! See, those are the cliffs straight ahead, and this right here is the Letter Lagoon."

"Eddie's right! Eddie's right!" Umber squealed with excitement.

"Well, what are we standing around for?" Alex piped in. "Let's follow the path!"

15

"Wait!" called Izzy as the others started off down the beach. "Shouldn't we gather some supplies?"

The Alpha-Maniacs stopped in their tracks. As usual, they knew Izzy was right.

"I'll grab the shovels," yelled Olly.

"And I'll get our pirate hats," called Alex.

"Don't forget the swords!" Eddie called after her.

The Alpha-Maniacs quickly loaded up their turtle wagon and set off down the path.

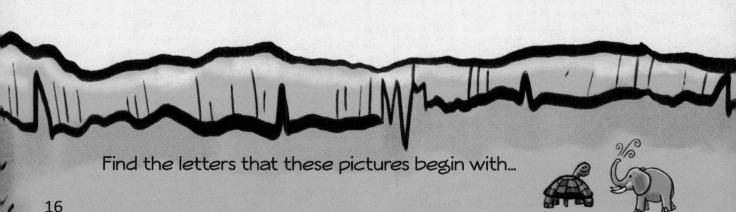

Find the letters that these pictures begin with...

The Alpha-Maniacs easily found the location of the X on the map. They had explored nearly every inch of Alpha-Mania Island.

"Nothing looks out of place here," remarked Izzy.

"Just start digging!" shouted Olly as he flung the shovels from the wagon.

Suddenly, a strange, deep voice echoed from the treetop.

"Ex...cuse me," murmured the voice. "Is some...one there?"

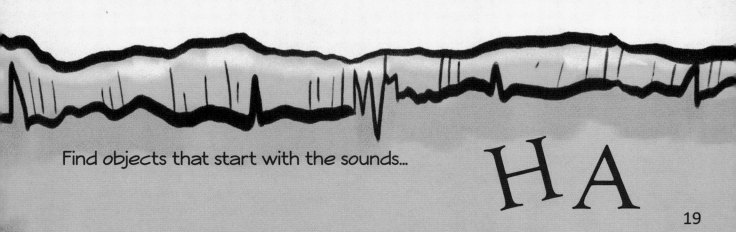

Find *objects* that start with the sounds...

HA

"Who said that?" asked Alex looking up.

"I diiid," answered the voice.

"Who, or what, are you?" demanded Eddie, puffing out his chest.

A furry gray sloth slid slowly down one of the tree branches.

"Mmmy nnnaaammme is Sssllllommmo the ssslllloth."

The Alpha-Maniacs looked bewildered.

"I think we're gonna need a translator," announced Olly. "This sloth speaks soooooo slowly!"

Can you help? What is the sloth's name?

"I ssseee you child...ren fffound my mmmaaap," Slomo muttered.

The Alpha-Maniacs stared blankly at the sloth. This was going to be a long day.

"Is there treasure buried here?" Olly asked, a little impatiently.

"There uuusssed to beee," slurred Slomo. "But I mmmoooved it."

"I don't understand a single thing this sloth says," grumbled Eddie. "How are we going to find this treasure?"

"It's easy, Eddie," explained Umber. "We just have to blend the sounds together to figure out the words he is saying."

"Ssso do you want to fffiiinnnd the treasure, thththennn?" inquired Slomo.

"We sure do!" squealed Alex. She was starting to catch on to the sloth's slow speech.

"Llliiisssten closely," continued Slomo, "First you mmmuuussst fol...low the rrrocks until you see a nnnessst."

"Follow the *who* until we see a *what*?" asked Olly.

"Listen," explained Umber, "He says it slowly —rrrocks — but we say it fast — rocks. Let's try the other one together. Slomo said 'nnnessst' so we say..."

"Nest!" shouted the Alpha-Maniacs.

"Don't worry, Olly." Umber stated confidently. "I know what to do."

With *Umber* leading the way, the Alpha-Maniacs soon arrived at a giant nest in a tiny tree.

"How do we get up there?" wondered Alex.

"C'mon *Umber*, I'll give you a boost," piped Eddie.

Umber groaned. He was always getting hoisted into unusual places.

Umber reached into the giant nest and pulled out another scroll.

"It's another note!" *Umber* cheered as he tumbled into a pile of moss.

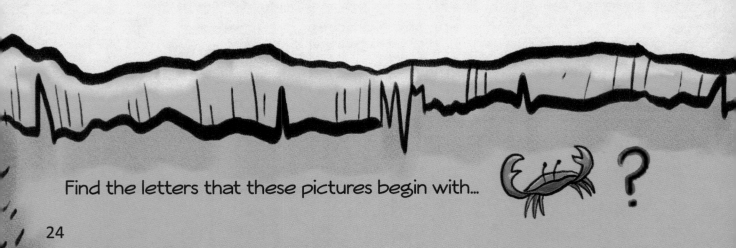

Find the letters that these pictures begin with... ?

As Umber brushed himself off, Alex read the note:

"Now follow the sssuuunnn until you rrreeeach,
The cllliiifffsss beyond the rrrocky beeeach."

Can you say it fast? Point to where the Alpha-Maniacs need to go next.

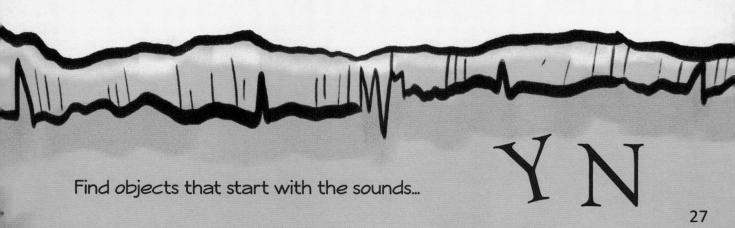

Find objects that start with the sounds...

Y N

When they reached the cliffs, the Alpha-Maniacs split up and began to search the rocky ground.

"I've got it!" announced Izzy, holding up another scroll.

She straightened her glasses and read the note:

"The letter S will lead you to
A lllaaake of many ffffiiish
Buried in the sssaaannnd beside
Is where you'll get your wish."

Where do the Alpha-Maniacs need to go next?"

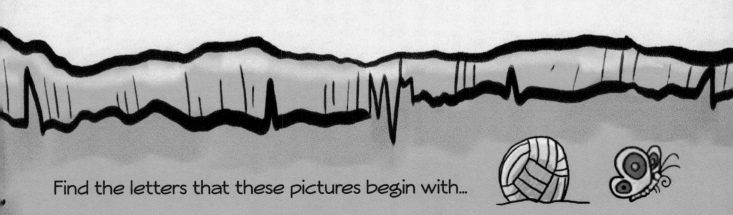

Find the letters that these pictures begin with...

With the help of some good blending, the Alpha-Maniacs arrived at the lake.

The excited Alpha-Maniacs dug furiously until Alex's shovel made a large bang.

"Over here! Over here!" Alex shrieked as she pulled out a small but heavy chest. Eddie used his shovel to pry it open.

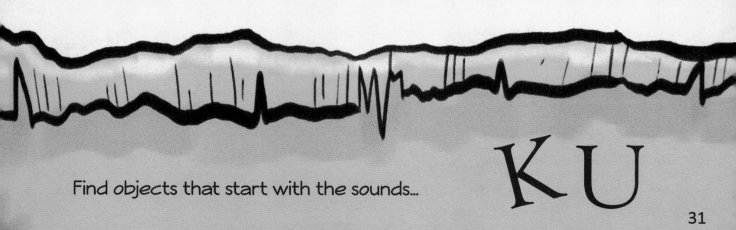

Find objects that start with the sounds...

$$KU$$

Inside the chest five gold crowns dotted with shimmering rubies, glimmering emeralds, and sparkling diamonds sat atop a sea of gleaming, gold coins.

As the Alpha-Maniacs stared in disbelief, Slomo slunk down a nearby tree trunk.

"Ex...cell...ent work child...ren. You have passed my t...est. You are worthy pro...tec...tors of my treasure."

"What do you mean, Slomo?" inquired Izzy.

"I've been search...ing for someone to help guard my treasure. You ssseee, I'm an old sssllloth and I'm too sssllow to keep mmmooovvving it."

"But why do you want to move it?" wondered Olly aloud. "Why not just keep it?"

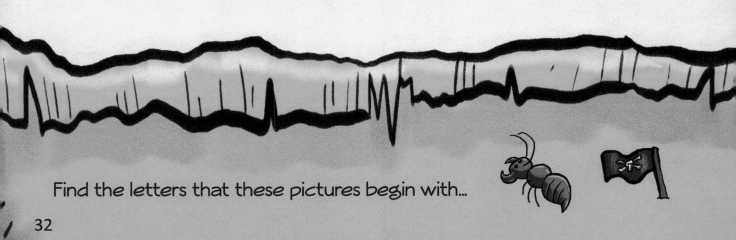

Find the letters that these pictures begin with...

"Well, there are two mmmaaapsss to this treasure. I have one, but the other fell into the hands of some greedy pirates. If I don't keep mmmooovvving the treasure, the greedy pirates will sure...ly fffiiinnnd it."

"We'll protect it! You can count on us, Slomo," assured Eddie.

"And in ex...change," answered Slomo, "I will give you half the treasure once we know it's sssaaafffe from the greedy pirates."

"Wow! Half of this treasure will be ours? You've got yourself a deal, sloth!" exclaimed Olly.

"Do you guys hear something?" Alex whispered.

The Alpha-Maniacs dropped their shovels and listened. A faint noise echoed off the nearby cliffs. It sounded like singing.

"That's a pirate song!" declared Eddie as the noise grew louder.

"Pirates?" Umber stammered nervously. "Which pirates?"

"Quick, bury the treasure!" shouted Olly, jumping into action.

The Alpha-Maniacs hurriedly buried Slomo's treasure and raced to the beach. An enormous, extravagant ship was heading straight for the Letter Lagoon.

"Quick, hide over here!" yelled Eddie, ducking behind a giant boulder.

The Alpha-Maniacs watched nervously as the mighty ship dropped its anchor. All of a sudden, an owl flew from the crow's nest and landed in front of the Alpha-Maniacs.

"I know that owl!" declared Alex. "He's a part of Captain Ray's crew!"

"Ahoy there, mateys!" bellowed a deep voice from the ship. "Have we got a story for ye fine landlubbers!"

The Alpha-Maniacs breathed a sigh of relief. Captain Ray and his crew had returned, just like they said they would. Slomo's treasure was safe...for now.

Additional Activities

Blending Activities

The following activities can easily be played with your child whenever you have a few minutes to spare. Blending activities are excellent ways to introduce your child to the idea that words are made up of individual sounds, which lays the foundation for reading and spelling skills down the road. All of the activities use objects you likely already have in the house or can easily obtain from a toy store or supermarket.

Head to Toe
(two or more players)

Setup:
Find a space where you and your child can spread out. Stand facing each other.

To Play:
This game allows your child to practice blending compound words and syllables together. Compound words are words that are made up of two or more smaller words. For example, the word *basketball* is a compound word because it consists of the smaller words *basket* and *ball*. Syllables are the parts of words that consist of a single, uninterrupted sound. For example, the word *dinosaur* has three syllables: *di-no-saur.*

Begin with compound words (See chart below). With your hands on your head, say the first part of the compound word aloud. As you bend down to touch your toes, say the final part of the compound word. (Parts of the compound word are separated with a dash.) Have your child repeat your actions and then try to call out the entire compound word without pausing.

When the compound words are complete, move on to syllables (See chart below). With your hands on your head, say the first syllable of the word. (Syllables are separated with dashes.) As you bend down to touch your toes, say the final syllable of the word. When the word contains three syllables, touch your head for the first syllable, your hips for the second syllable, and your toes for the final syllable. Have your child repeat your actions and then try to call out the entire word without pausing.

Compound Words	Syllables
no-where	rock-et
air-port	pi-rate
paint-brush	din-ner
bath-tub	chick-en
break-fast	el-e-phant
drive-way	fam-i-ly
eye-brow	ham-bur-ger
pine-cone	com-pu-ter

Leap Frog
(two or more players)

Setup:
Find a space where you and your child can spread out. Lay out two mats or mark the floor to show two boxes in a vertical line from where you are standing.

To Play:
This game allows your child to practice blending the onset and rime of words. The onset of a word refers to the beginning sound or sounds up to the first vowel. For example, the onset of the word *green* is */gr/.* The rime of a word refers to the remaining part of the word. For example, the rime of the word *green* is */een/.* Model for your child how to use the mats to help blend the onset and rime of a word by doing the following: Hop onto the first mat and say the onset of a word (See chart below). Next, hop onto the second mat and say the rime of a word. Finally, hop off the mat and say the word in its entirety. Now allow your child to take a turn hopping. As your child hops to the first mat, call out an onset and have your child repeat it after you. As your child hops to the next mat, call out the rime and have your child repeat it after you. Then encourage your child to hop off the mat and call out the word in its entirety.

Onset	Rime	Entire Word
/b/	/irthday/	Birthday
/c/	/ookie/	Cookie
/j/	/ump/	Jump
/m/	/ap/	Map
/ch/	/est/	Chest
/sh/	/ip/	Ship
/bl/	/ack/	Black
/str/	/ap/	Strap

Find it Fast
(two or more players)

To Play:
As you flip through the book with your child, call out the name of an object on the page by stretching the individual sounds. Have your child point to the object as quickly as he or she can. Choose objects from the following list as they contain stretchy sounds that are easier to blend. Remember: Only hold the sounds that are written multiple times. Do not hold final sounds like /ck/, /p/, /t/, etc.

Sun (Say "Sssssssuuuuuunnnnnn")

Leaves (Say "Llllllleeeeeeeavvvvvves")

Nail (Say "Nnnnnnaaaaaaaillllll")

Fish (Say "Fffffffiiiiiish")

Map (Say "Mmmmmmaaaaaap")

Snake (Say "Ssssssssnnnnnnaaaaaaake")

Flag (Say "Ffffffllllllaaaaaag")

Feet (Say "Fffffffeeeeeeeeeeet")

Slomo Says, "Say It Fast"
(two or more players)

To Play:

This game allows you and your child to practice blending compound words, syllables, and individual sounds. Tell your child that you are going to pretend to be Slomo the Sloth and say words very "ssslllowly". Your child will then have to say it fast. Choose words from the following list. Start with compound words, then move on to syllables, followed by two-phoneme words, three-phoneme words, and finally four-phoneme words. Remember to pause at the breaks in compound words, between syllables, and to hold only the individual sounds that are written multiple times. Do not hold final sounds such as /ck/, /p/, /g/, and /t/.

Compound Words:	Syllables:	Individual Sounds (Phonemes):
Neck-lace	Ro-bot	**Two-Phoneme Words:**
Pass-word	Ten-nis	Aaaaaat (At)
In-side	Pig-let	Uuuuuup (Up)
Base-ball	Pup-pet	Zzzzzzoo (Zoo)
Door-knob	Mu-sic	Mmmmmmeeeeee (Me)
Fish-bowl	Win-dow	Iiiiiiffffff (If)
Bed-time	Ba-by	**Three-Phoneme Words:**
Foot-print	Can-dy	Rrrrrraaaaaake (Rake)
Hair-cut	Cu-cum-ber	Vvvvvvaaaaaannnnnn (Van)
Grape-fruit	Um-brel-la	Sssssssiiiiiit (Sit)
Key-board	For-get-ful	Nnnnnneeeeeeeat (Neat)
Life-guard	Sat-ur-day	Lllllliiiiiip (Lip)
Mail-box	Fan-tas-tic	**Four-Phoneme Words:**
Pan-cake	Un-der-stand	Ffffffllllllliiiiiip (Flip)
Play-ground	No-vem-ber	Sssssslllllliiiiiide (Slide)
Rain-bow	Mac-a-ro-ni	Fffffaaaaaasssssst (Fast)
Shoe-lace	Kin-der-gar-ten	Lllllaaaaaammmmmmp (Lamp)
Tip-toe	In-for-ma-tion	Sssssssmmmmmmaaaaash (Smash)

Phonics Activities

The following activities practice phonics, or sound/symbol correspondence. You can help your child learn both the names of letters and the sounds they make by playing games that emphasize the initial sounds in words. Have a set of alphabet letters on hand so that you can reinforce the symbol that each sound represents. This could be magnetic letters, alphabet puzzle pieces, alphabet flashcards, or any letters your child can hold in his or her hand. Playing with three-dimensional letters will help your child better understand the concept of letters as symbols for sounds.

It Starts With a...
(two or more players)

Setup:
Find a variety of small objects or toys from around the house. The objects should be familiar to your child and begin with letters that make their usual sound. For example, do not use a "phone" because children should learn that *p* says /p/ as in *pot* before they learn that *ph* says /f/. Try to choose multiple objects that begin with the same sound. Also, have a set of alphabet letters beside you.

To Play:
Lay out the objects on the floor between you and your child. Review the name of each object with your child. Hold up an alphabet letter and tell your child the name of the letter and the sound it makes. ("This is the letter B. It makes the sound /b/.") It is important to pronounce the sounds of letters correctly. Please see Appendix A for a guide to letter sounds. Explain to your child that you are going to sing a song to help your child find an object that begins with the letter/sound you are holding. Sing the following song to the tune of *The Farmer in the Dell*:

It starts with a... (Call out the sound of the letter you are holding)
It starts with a... (Call out the sound of the letter you are holding)
Pick it up and hold it if it starts with a... (Call out the sound of the letter you are holding)

While you are singing, your child should look for an object that begins with the correct sound. When the song ends, discuss the object your child chose and why it begins or does not begin with the letter and sound you are holding. Put that object aside and repeat with other letters until most of the objects have been removed.

Musical Letters
(two or more players)

Setup:
Lay out some alphabet letters in a large circle on the floor. Choose an area where you have access to music and room to spread out.

To Play:
Have your child start by standing on one of the letters. Review each letter on the floor by saying the name of the letter and the sound it makes. ("This is the letter T, it makes the sound /t/.") Start the music and have your child march around the circle stepping on each letter. If you have a remote control for your music source, you can march around the circle with your child. Choose a point to stop the music and instruct your child to stop and stand on the nearest letter. Have your child say the name of the letter and the sound it makes. You can also get your child to name something that begins with that sound. Once your child is successful, start the music again and continue. Try to ensure that your child has a chance to practice each letter in the circle.

Appendix A -
Guide to Letter Sounds

- There are two main types of sounds (also called *phonemes*) in the English language: voiced sounds and unvoiced sounds.

- *Voiced sounds* occur when the vocal chords vibrate in order to produce the sound. To test this, put your fingers gently against your throat below your chin. As you say a voiced sound, you should feel a gentle vibration against your fingers.

- *Unvoiced sounds* (also called *whisper sounds*) do not use the vocal chords. For an unvoiced sound, put your fingers a short distance from your mouth. As you say an unvoiced sound, you should feel a slight puff of air against your fingers. Unvoiced sounds are often incorrectly pronounced as voiced sounds. This results in the vowel sound /uh/ following the letter sound, which is incorrect. For example, the letter *P* should sound like a whisper or puff of air (/p/, not /puh/).

- Sounds can also be "quick" or "stretchy."Stretchy sounds are those that should be held when pronounced (/mmmm/).Quick sounds should not be held (/t/).

The following chart illustrates the voiced and unvoiced sounds along with the quick and stretchy sounds.

Voiced		Unvoiced	
Quick	**Stretchy**	**Quick**	**Stretchy**
b (/b/ as in bed)	a (/aaaa/ as in apple)	c (/c/ as in cat)	f (/ffff/ as in find)
d (/d/ as in dog)	e (/eeee/ as in egg)	h (/h/ as in hat)	s (/ssss/ as in sun)
g (/g/ as in go)	i (/iiii/ as in igloo)	k (/k/ as in kite)	
j (/j/ as in jet)	l (/llll/ as in lion)	p (/p/ as in pet)	
q (/kw/ as in quit)	m (/mmmm/ as in map)	t (/t/ as in time)	
w (/w/ as in wet)	n (/nnnn/ as in net)	x (/ks/ as in bo<u>x</u>)	
y (/y/ as in yellow)	o (/oooo/ as in octopus)		
	r (/rrrr/ as in rock)		
	u (/uuuu/ as in umbrella)		
	v (/vvvv/ as in van)		
	z (/zzzz/ as in zoo)		

Endnotes

1   Andrea A. Zevenbergen and Grover J. Whitehurst, "Dialogic Reading: A Shared Picture Book Reading Intervention for Preschoolers," *On Reading Books to Children: Parents and Teachers*, ed. Anne van Kleeck, et al. (Mahwah, NJ: Lawrence Erlbaum Associates, Inc., 2000), 177.

2   National Institute for Literacy, *Report of the National Reading Panel. Put Reading First: The Research Building Blocks for Teaching Children to Read*, 2000.

3   Ontario Ministry of Education, *Early Reading Strategy: The Report of the Expert Panel on Early Reading in Ontario* (Toronto: Queen's Printer for Ontario, 2003).

4   Lita Ericson and Moira Fraser Juliebo, *The Phonological Awareness Handbook for Kindergarten and Primary Teachers* (Newark, DE: International Reading Association, 1998), 5.

5   Linnea C. Ehri and Theresa Roberts, "The Roots of Learning to Read and Write: Acquisition of Letters and Phonemic Awareness," *Handbook of Early Literacy Research,* Volume 2, ed. David K. Dickenson and Susan B. Neuman (New York: Guilford Press, 2006), 113–30.

6   Nancy K. Lewkowicz, "Phonemic Awareness Training: What to Teach and How to Teach It," *Journal of Educational Psychology* 72, no. 5 (1980): 686.

7   National Institute for Literacy, *Report of the National Reading Panel. Put Reading First: The Research Building Blocks for Teaching Children to Read*, 2000.

8   Lita Ericson and Moira Fraser Juliebo, *The Phonological Awareness Handbook for Kindergarten and Primary Teachers* (Newark, DE: International Reading Association, 1998), 53.

9   Anthony D. Fredericks, *The Complete Phonemic Awareness Handbook* (Wilmington, MA: Houghton Mifflin Harcourt, 2001), 20.

Made in the USA
Charleston, SC
18 February 2016